Christmas 2006

Dear Mom & Dad —
    to provide a little
more context for your local
explorations — as I know
you certainly don't need
more inspiration!
        Love,

        Anne

STELLENBOSCH

La Compagnie du Cap cc
P O Box 15726, Vlaeberg 8018
lacompag@iafrica.com

Registration number CK9501664/07
First published in South Africa in 2006

Concept and Editor: Daniel A. Pennewaert
Editorial advisor: Marje Hemp

Contributors:
Layout: Julie Habbouche
Typography and cover design: Ernst-Reiner Klaus
Proof-reader: Mary Simpson

Reproduction: Photoplate Digital Prepress, Cape Town
Printed and bound by Mills Litho (Ltd), Cape Town

ISBN 0 620 35009 1

Burgherhuis, side gable   Burgherhuis, front gable   Cottage, Herte Street   Clockwise from top left:

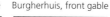

Along Adam Tas Road;
The Café Cat*, Plein Street;
67 Victoria Street;
Water furrow, Van Riebeeck Street

*Sculpted by Nerine Desmond (1950) to
commemorate an official decision that
cats should not be allowed in restaurants
in Stellenbosch.

STELLENBOSCH

A NATION WITHOUT HISTORY IS LIKE SOMEONE WITHOUT A MEMORY.
HISTORICALLY BUILDINGS SYMBOLIZE HISTORY.
THEY ARE THE VISIBLE FOOTPRINT OF OUR CULTURAL HERITAGE.

Dr Anton Rupert, *1916 – 2006*
Former founder and chairman of Historical Homes of South Africa

Stellenbosch, the second oldest town in South Africa, is also one of the best preserved. It is the epitomy of beauty and splendour, combining elegant architecture with oak-lined streets and white-washed façades etched against blue skies. The town has succeeded in changing across the eras without sacrificing its soul and it boasts some of the best examples of restored historical buildings in the Cape. While some buildings have been left intact over the years, the majority have been lovingly and authentically restored.

Founded in 1679 by Simon van der Stel soon after his arrival at the Cape, the tiny settlement on the banks of the Eerste River slowly transformed itself into a frontier town, where law and order were upheld, taxes were instituted and religion played a major role. A magistracy was established in 1685 by the Dutch East India Company and the *landdrost* wielded enormous power over its citizens and the denizens of the unknown territory beyond.

The original houses were single-storeyed with wooden beams and thick-walls built of sun-dried bricks, which were mud-lined inside and finished with a protective lime-wash on the outside. The size of the rooms initially depended on the roofing materials available locally hence they were lofty but narrow. Streets were lined with burbling furrows bringing water to every household and shady oaks were planted, hence its name *Eikestad* or 'town of oaks'.

In the early 1700s Cape Dutch-style gables became very fashionable. Modelled on baroque architecture found in Holland during the 17th and 18th centuries, Cape Dutch became uniquely South African with its elegantly symmetrical proportions and central decorative gable. The intricate plaster work on the gable often incorporates a founding date.

It was only in the later part of the 18th century, in spite of several disastrous fires that ravaged the settlement, that the town of Stellenbosch grew and prospered sufficiently for grander double-storeyed houses to be built and smaller dwellings to be expanded.

During the 19th century Regency, Cape Georgian, neo-classic Renaissance and Victorian styles came into vogue and these classic styles can all be seen in Stellenbosch today. A walk down Dorp street, originally the old wagon road to the Cape, will show Dutch gables, Georgian façades and fanciful Victorian turrets. Side streets often culminate interestingly in dignified historic buildings or lead on to the Braak. A visit to the Stellenbosch Village Museum is worthwhile as the complex, comprising four meticulously restored houses, illustrates the different architectural styles, furnishings and gardens during the three centuries of Stellenbosch's existence.

Today Stellenbosch is the centre of South Africa's wine and viticulture industry and embraces Stellenbosch University, one of the oldest centres of higher learning in South Africa. Although the university was established in 1918, the original Victoria College was founded in 1881.

Stellenbosch is usually bustling with students and tourists alike, enjoying an olde worlde, unhurried atmosphere. After spending time in Stellenbosch, you will leave with many memories of an historic town surrounded by oaks, vineyards and gables.

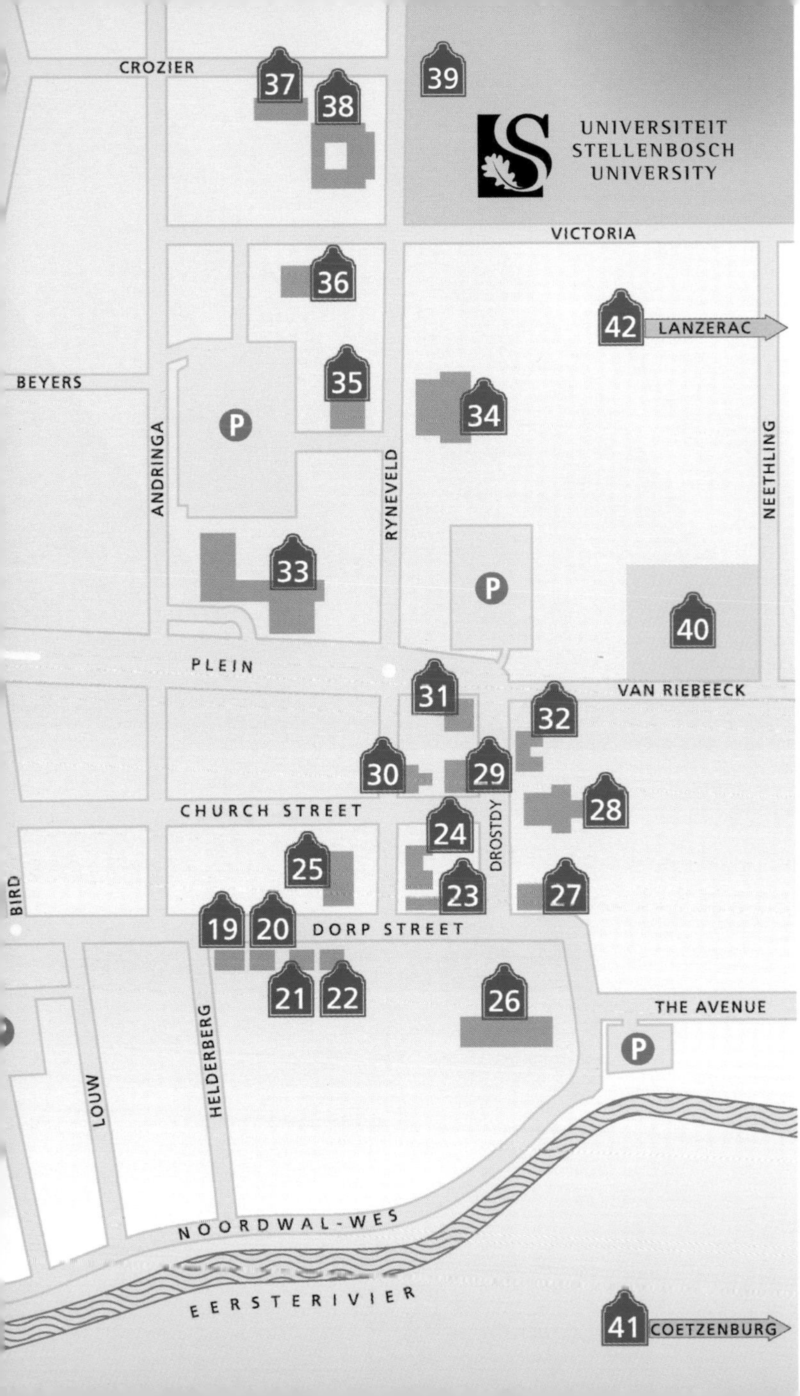
CROZIER
37
38
39
UNIVERSITEIT
STELLENBOSCH
UNIVERSITY
VICTORIA
36
42
LANZERAC
BEYERS
35
P
34
ANDRINGA
RYNEVELD
NEETHLING
33
P
40
PLEIN
31
VAN RIEBEECK
32
30
29
28
CHURCH STREET
24
DROSTDY
25
23
27
BIRD
19
20
DORP STREET
21
22
26
THE AVENUE
P
LOUW
HELDERBERG
NOORDWAL-WES
EERSTERIVIER
41
COETZENBURG

CONTENTS

▲

An ancient wooden grape press draws attention to the restored Libertas Parva complex in lower Dorp Street. Since the arrival of the French Huguenots in 1688, Stellenbosch has remained central to the Cape's celebrated winelands.

▶

KRIGE HOUSES *c.1783*
25-33 Dorp Street

The early houses of Stellenbosch were often single-storeyed, thatched and gabled as seen in this annexe of small dwelling units adjoining Libertas Parva.

◀ ◀

Previous page

Crimson bougainvilleas *(left)* adorn the entrance of Distell's headquarters on Adam Tas Road. Across the way nestles the cottage of Mon Repos c.1848 *(right)*, so named by a French silversmith who couldn't pronounce its earlier title *Onder Papegaaiberg*.

◄ ►

LIBERTAS PARVA *c.1783*
KLEIN LIBERTAS
25-33 Dorp Street

This classic H-shaped homestead with its early unadorned gable was built by Lambertus Fick in 1783 and restored by Historical Homes of South Africa in 1970. Framed by moulded pilasters and a central neoclassical pediment, the two front doors create a pleasing façade, although only one of the doors is functional. The other has been included for balance.

▶

Cape Dutch architecture is renowned for its elegance and symmetry as seen in this pre-1800 dormer gable framing the moulded wooden door and fanlight at the rear of Libertas Parva. Today this complex now houses offices of the Distell group.

KRIGE COTTAGES *c.1900*
37-51 Dorp Street

This row of semi-detached cottages
in lower Dorp Street, erected in 1850,
was remodelled and Victorianized in
1900 with dormer windows *(above)*,
simple cast-iron verandas and corrugated
iron roofs.

14

▲ ▶
ROOKSKIP
Corner Dorp and Papegaai streets

When an outbuilding on the farm De Hoop was converted into a row of semi-detached cottages *(above)* the tall, upright chimneys (since removed) resembled the funnels of a steam ship hence the name, *rookskip* or 'smoke stacks'. Striking archways *(right)* interlink to support the shady front stoep.

ACKERMANN HOUSE *1815*
48-50 Dorp Street

This house fronting lower Dorp Street is an excellent example of meticulous restoration. During his student days Jan Christiaan Smuts lodged here with Mrs Ackermann, at a time when the house was Victorianized and much altered. It has since been restored and given this beautiful neoclassical gable *(right)*.

▶

ACKERMANN HOUSE *1815*
48-50 Dorp Street

The classic proportions of an H-shaped, Cape Dutch-style home, typical of many manor houses in the Stellenbosch area, are clearly seen in this side and rear view of Ackermann House.

▶ ▶

Following page

VREDELUST *1814*
63 Dorp Street

Set well back from Dorp Street and surrounded by a low werf wall, this restored homestead possesses an unsual low balustrade. Built along the top of the front wall it prevents rainwater from dripping down the façade. The land on which the homestead stands was part of the farm Libertas, owned by the redoubtable Free Burgher and diarist, Adam Tas, back in the earliest days of Stellenbosch.

◄

OOM SAMIE SE WINKEL
1904
82-84 Dorp Street

The cluttered interior of Oom Samie se Winkel *(left)*, an old-fashioned shop reminiscent of a rural general dealer's store at the turn of the 20th century, is now a popular tourist attraction in Dorp Street.

▶

HERTE STREET COTTAGES
c.1838
25-35 Herte Street

A terrace of modest cottages *(right)* built by missionary teacher Jacob Schultz to house slaves freed after 1834. The iron roofs were once thatched.

▲

HERTE STREET COTTAGES
c.1838
25-35 Herte Street

Each cottage *(above)* on the west side of Herte Street is graced with a small, straight-sided gable. The cottages are situated opposite the gardens of the old Rhenish Parsonage *(right)*.

▶

RHENISH PARSONAGE *c.1815*
36 Market Street

The original parsonage, once home to Reverend Lückhoff, was destroyed by fire in 1909 and has been completely rebuilt. The new building with its classic gable, small triangular pediment and almost perfect proportions is set in spacious surroundings with an old mill-stream running nearby.

▶

BURGHERHUIS *1797*
Alexander Street

The original building was a narrow
H-shape homestead with holbol end
gables and shuttered windows *(right).*
The house was in a state of disrepair
before being restored by Historical
Homes of South Africa to serve as their
headquarters. Several rooms are open
to the public to view the Cape furniture,
porcelain and glassware.

◀ ◀

Previous page

The Burgherhuis was built by Anthonie
Fick on land granted to him towards the
end of the 18th century. Later it was
occupied by the Reverend Lückhoff of
the Rhenish Missionary Society whose
church was nearby on the west side
of the Braak. The back gable is a more
modern addition to this beautifully
restored homestead, as is the pergola,
but the vine is of very old stock.

◀

BURGHERHUIS *1797*
40 Bloem Street

The front gable of the Burgherhuis *(left)*, decorated with plaster swags and an urn, is one of the oldest and finest examples of a neo-classical gable in Stellenbosch. Also dating from the 18th century is this fine stable-type front door set in an architrave of brick and plaster.

▶

COACHMAN'S COTTAGE
c.1791
LANKHOFF COTTAGE
40 Alexander Street

An early example of a dormer gable above the stable-type door graces this charming cottage *(right)*. Built by Jan Gorg Lankhoff, a German tailor, for his family in the late 18th century, it was partially destroyed in a storm and later restored. Together with the Burgherhuis and Kruithuis, it now forms part of an attractive group of historical buildings situated near the Braak.

▲ ▶

V.O.C. KRUITHUIS *1777*
ARSENAL
The Braak

The thick-walled, barrel-vaulted arsenal was built to store ammunition for the protection of the tiny settlement. Today it is the only existing national monument bearing the V.O.C. inscription of the Dutch East India Company.

◄

RHENISH INSTITUTE *1862*
3 Bloem Street

The original H-shaped homestead, built in 1787 on the farm De Oude Molen, was a single-storeyed, thatched dwelling. It was acquired in 1862 by the Rhenish missionaries and used as a boarding house for girls who attended the local Rhenish school. Later on it was extended to accommodate more pupils and given an upper storey with a flat roof. Today it is used as the P J Olivier Art Centre.

35

◀ ▲

RHENISH MISSION CHURCH
1823
Bloem Street

Situated at the southern end of the Braak, the Rhenish Church is one of the oldest and most beautiful of the country's churches. In 1829 the German Rhenish Mission Society sent out the Reverend Lückhoff to Stellenbosch. He took over a small building, originally built in 1823 and owned by the Dutch Reformed Church. After the emancipation of slaves, the church was considerably enlarged in 1840 to house its burgeoning congregation. The decorative gable *(above)* bears the date from this time. Later two church bells were mounted in a double-arched bell tower *(left)*. Much has changed over the years, but the church still stands at the heart of the Rhenish complex.

▲ ▶
VOORGELEGEN *c.1798*
116 Dorp Street

This fine example of a flat-roofed, double storey house in Cape Georgian style *(right)* used to be single storeyed, thatched and gabled. The bracketed moulding above the decorative fanlight prevents rainwater from dripping down the façade. Today it houses a miniature and toy museum *(above)*.

◀ ◀
Previous page

Many homes in Dorp Street show decorative fanlights above the front door that allow additional light into an otherwise gloomy interior.

▲ ▶

LA GRATITUDE   *1798*
95 Dorp Street

This is possibly the best known house in Dorp Street, not because of its perfectly proportioned façade with its classical gable, but for the unusual bas relief above the gable window – the all seeing eye of the Almighty *(above)*.

▶ ▶

Following page
Details of La Gratitude's escutcheon plate on the front door *(left)*.

42

◄

THE CORNER HOUSE *1830*
149 Dorp Street

This elegant 19th century gabled home *(left)* occupies a prominent corner site and reflects the architectural style of Stellenbosch two centuries ago. All historical buildings in Stellenbosch carry the distinctive plaque of the National Monuments Council *(above)*.

◄ ◄

Previous page

STELLENBOSCH GYMNASIUM *1866*
120-122 Dorp Street

Originally built as a place of learning to provide boys with a higher education, the Stellenbosch Gymnasium at one time accommodated both the Paul Roos Gymnasium and the Victoria College, later to become Stellenbosch University. Seen here is the unusual covered porch with neo-gothic tracery.

◀

HAUPTFLEISCH HOUSE *1812*
153 Dorp Street

This house, partially renovated by Historical Homes of South Africa in 1997, once had a dormer front gable and holbol end gables (seen here left of the roof line). In 1860 the thatch was removed and eaves were raised thus altering the structure of the building so that the front gable could no longer be fully restored. The replacement corrugated iron roof has been left intact.

▶

LOUBSER HOUSE *1825*
157 Dorp Street

The house itself is 18th century and until 1824 it served as a parsonage for the Stellenbosch Missionary Society. A small chapel was situated behind. In 1825 the small front gable with overlapping roundels on the pilasters was added.

SAXENHOF *1890*
159 Dorp Street

This early house, named after free burgher and tanner Peter Saxe, is depicted in a 1710 panorama of the village. The present double-storey house with its elaborate Victorian balcony dates from 1890 and was left intact during its restoration by Historic Homes of South Africa.

KOLONIESHUIS *1694*
2 Ryneveld Street

This 'colony house' may well be one of the oldest buildings still standing in Stellenbosch. Its foundations date to a few years after Stellenbosch was founded. The T-shaped house has a steeply-pitched roof and an unusual pointed front gable.

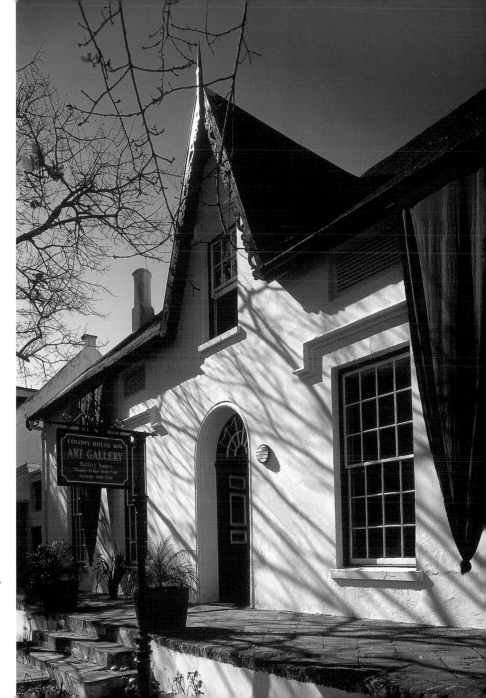

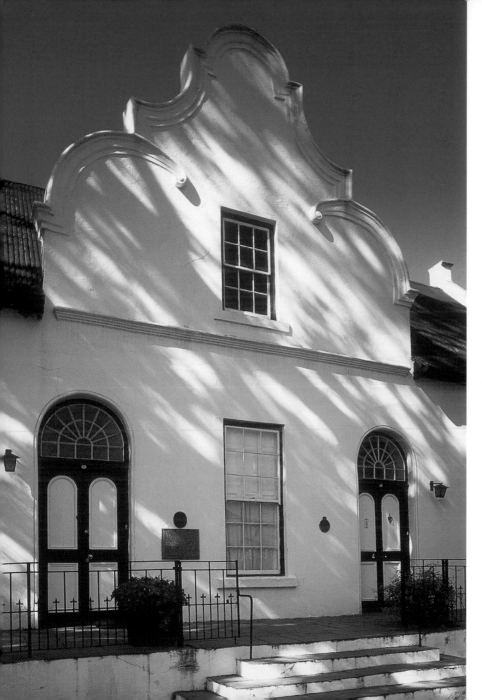

◄

MORKEL HOUSE *c.1700*
4-6 Ryneveld Street

This building was originally a wine cellar before being requisitioned as a place of worship after the devastating fire of 1710. In the1890s the property was purchased by Mr D.C. Morkel (hence the name). The front holbol gable was reconstructed in the late 1960s to match the original side gable dating back to 1775. The pair of Victorian front doors and slate-paved stoep were kept intact.

►

HOFMEYR HALL *1899*
39 Church Street

The classical architecture of this hall is synonymous with the Greek revival style of the Victorian era. It was named after a Theology professor N. J. Hofmeyr and serves as a missionary centre where works of art are occasionally exhibited.

THEOLOGICAL SEMINARY
1905-1920 (present form)
KWEEKSKOOL
Dorp Street

The ornate Theological Seminary occupies the historic site of Simon van der Stel's first encampment on an island in the Eerste River and where Stellenbosch's first public building was erected. The old Drostdy, dating back to 1687, housed the first landdrost and magistrate's court. In 1853 the property was taken over by the Dutch Reformed Church and in 1859 it became the first institution of higher learning in Stellenbosch. A second storey, designed by architect Carl Otto Hager, was added in 1905 and in the 1920s it was converted into its current imposing French baroque style.

CHURCH HOUSE *1753-1787*
UTOPIA
Corner Drostdy and Dorp streets

This H-shaped homestead has undergone
many changes since it was built by Philip
Hartog between 1753 and 1787. It has
been magnificently restored and since
1961 it has been used as the Dutch
Reformed Church Council offices. Gabled
burial vaults in the foreground lie in the
Moederkerk cemetery. The origin of the
gable with its palm tree fresco *(above)*
is uncertain.

▷

MOEDERKERK *1863 (present form)*
DUTCH REFORMED MOTHER CHURCH
Drostdy Street

The neo-gothic interior of the Moederkerk
shows its high ceilings, domed chancel
and tall, carved pulpit (the fourth in the
church's history). After the original building
was destroyed in the great fire of 1710,
the church was rebuilt on its present site.
In 1863 it was enlarged and altered by
the famous German master builder and
architect Carl Otto Hager.

▷ ▷

O.M. BERGH-HUIS
c.1838 (present form)
Village Museum
Corner Drostdy and Church streets

This Cape Georgian double-storey building
(opposite) with its wide, triangular
pediment and sash windows was occupied
by the family of Olof Bergh, descendant
of the famous Swedish explorer. The rich
interior of the house, with its formal heavy
furnishings, flocked wallpaper and sombre
paintings, depicts the Cape-Victorian way
of life in Stellenbosch between 1840-1880.

58

SCHREUDERHUIS *1709*
Village Museum
18 Ryneveld Street

This humble thatched cottage is the oldest dwelling in Stellenbosch and is now part of the Village Museum.
It dates back to the original settlement and is one of the few buildings to have survived the devastating fire of 1710. Although much altered over the years, the cottage has been faithfully restored with unglazed windows, thick clay walls, *misvloer* and handmade wooden furniture showing the austere living conditions of the original settlers.

◄

BLETTERMANHUIS *1789*
Village Museum
Corner Drostdy and Plein streets

An elegant H-shaped Cape Dutch
manor house with beautiful period
furniture and tiled entrance hall
(previous page) illustrates the life of
a well off family in the later part
of the 18ᵗʰ century. It was built by
Hendrik Lodewijk Bletterman, the
last Stellenbosch *landdrost* appointed
by the V.O.C. The beautifully
proportioned rear of the house *(left)*
overlooks an old-fashioned garden.

▶ ▶

Following page
GROSVENOR HOUSE *1782*
Village Museum
10-14 Drostdy Street

Grosvenor House is one of the finest
and grandest examples of the Cape
Georgian period in Stellenbosch.
Fluted pilasters flank the *'bo-en-onder'*
teak door, and in the triangular
pediment above is a stylised palm tree
used as a seal by the Stellenbosch
Dutch Reformed Church and the
Village Museum. It is furnished to
depict the fashions of an upper-class
English colonial family from 1800 1830.
The walls of the *voorkamer (left)* have
been restored by marbelling, a paint
finish popular in the early 19ᵗʰ century

◄

VICTORIAN COTTAGES c.1850
Corner Drostdy and Plein streets

These semi-detatched cottages are typical of the late 19th century trend of Victorianization popular in many Boland towns. The thatch was removed and the pitch of the roof was altered, thus heightening the walls. Small windows or louvred air vents were often built into the extra space to allow light and air into the loft. Fashionable verandas were created to keep the façades cool and protect them from the elements. Beyond stands Blettermanhuis. Its flamboyant restored gable *(above)* is 18th century baroque in style.

◄ ◄
Previous page

TOWN HALL *1941*
Plein Street

This imposing complex of public
buildings was built in the neo-Cape
Dutch and Classical Revival styles
with all their embellishments and
flourishes.

◄ ►

BLOEMHOF GIRLS' SCHOOL
1907
32 Ryneveld Street

The imposing façade of this red
brick building with its three-tiered
Dutch neo-Rennaissance gables
dates back to 1907. The school
was founded in1875 with the
establishment of the Bloemhof
Seminary for Girls in Dorp Street.
When the school outgrew its
premises it moved here and today
it houses the Sasol Art Museum.

◄ ▲
ERFURT HOUSE   *1876*
37 Ryneveld Street

This beautiful square house built in the German *Jugendstiel* with its decorative wood and wrought iron balcony and ornate fountain *(above)* is an example of the late Victorian style of architecture. In 1991 it was purchased by the Stellenbosch Village Museum and is now in use as its administration headquarters and houses a library.

◄ ◄

Previous page

CROZIER HOUSE *c1900*
11 Victoria Street

This classical façade incorporates both
Georgian and Victorian features. The
double-storeyed building was erected
at the turn of the century to house
students for Victoria College, forerunner
to Stellenbosch University.

◄

SEMI-DETATCHED COTTAGES
1895
16-24 Crozier Street

This short terrace of Victorian semi-
detached cottages with their tiny
gardens, fretted bargeboards and
pointed dormer windows typifies the
true village atmosphere of the 1900s.

▶

C.L. MARAIS LIBRARY *1899*
Crozier Street

Neo-Classical and neo-Renaissance
in style, this ornate late Victorian
building is one of only two academic
buildings surviving from Victoria
College days. It was originally erected
as a library, the first building for this
purpose in South Africa.

VICTORIA COLLEGE *1886*
OU HOOFGEBOU
Ryneveld Street

One of Stellenbosch's distinctive academic structures, it was built in classic Greek Revival style to commemorate the bicentennial of Stellenbosch. It was renamed Victoria College of Stellenbosch in 1887 in celebration of Queen Victoria's 50 years of rule.

▶ ▶

Following page

The Stellenbosch University campus *(left)* dates back to 1918 and today it offers a wide range of degree courses and numerous diplomas. Students seek out peace and tranquility under the dappled shade of exotic trees in the University's botanical gardens *(right)* in Neethling Street. The gardens are renowned for their unusual plant collections.

Previous page

VICTORIAN TURRETS *c.1900*
Van Riebeeck Street

A group of late Victorian villas in Van Riebeeck Street shows a very distinctive architectural style with their fretwork bargeboard gables and decorative cast iron *broekie lace* mouldings *(left)*, corner turrets with pointed steeples *(centre)*, and onion domes *(right)*.

◀ ▶
COETZENBURG
1893 (present form)
Coetzenburg Street

This historic H-plan homestead on the banks of the Eerste River was completely Victorianized in a grand extravaganza at the turn of the century. The front gable was destroyed and the façade adorned with an elaborate fretwork veranda and balcony in multiple patterns. Today it houses the university sports offices and club. In front stands an imposing statue *(left)* of rugby legend Dr Daniel Hartman Craven (1910-1993) and his dog *'Bliksem'*.

▶ ▶
Following page
LANZERAC *1830*
Lanzerac Street

One of Stellenbosch's oldest farms, the land on which Lanzerac stands today was granted to Isaac Schryver in 1692. In 1808 it was purchased by Coenraad Johannes Fick and it was he who completed the gabled manor house in 1830. This elegant Cape Dutch homestead, set against the majestic Jonkershoek peaks, is now a well-known hotel. The front gable is typically neo-classical in style with pediment, tall pilasters surmounted by vases, and well-defined mouldings.